EISENHOWER

B
92   FABER
Eis
c.1   Dwight Eisenhower

X

DWIGHT EISENHOWER

President Dwight D. Eisenhower.

DWIGHT EISENHOWER

DORIS FABER

Illustrated with Photographs

Abelard–Schuman
New York

For Hal

CONTENTS

1 GANDER AND DANDER

It was a mean bird, he could tell by its hissing.

But Dwight really wanted to look around this whole barnyard, and no goose was going to stop him. So he kept walking, step after step, while the goose strutted right toward him.

Then, suddenly, fierce feathers were surrounding him, and the little boy began running, bawling loudly. Not that he was scared—no, he was plain mad, he blubbered when Uncle Luther came out to rescue him.

In that case, said his uncle, he had an idea. Fetching an old broom, he cut off part of the handle and most of the straw. What was left made a sort of club with a padded end, easy for a small boy to carry.

"Now let's see if that tough old gander bothers you again," Uncle Luther said.

Sure enough, the big bird started strutting over the minute Dwight emerged from the back door. Holding

1

the broom, the boy advanced a little nervously. But before the gander could attack, Dwight did.

He let out a yell and rushed forward, waving the broom. The hissing changed to a squawk of alarm. This time, the small boy chased the big bird! During the rest of Dwight's visit, he did his exploring without any further trouble. He brought along the broom, though, to be on the safe side.

Dwight David Eisenhower was not quite five years old then, when he stayed a few weeks at a Kansas farm owned by some relatives. Many years later, he liked to tell people that the first thing he could remember was that mean gander and the lesson it had taught him: Don't ever try to deal with an enemy unless you're strong enough to beat him.

Yet he didn't have the slightest notion of becoming a soldier while he was growing up. Because his father had worked briefly for a railroad, he'd been born down in Texas—on October 14, 1890. A tiny frame house facing the railroad tracks in the dusty town of Denison would turn into a tourist attraction a long time afterward, with a sign out front labeling it as his birthplace. But he was still an infant when his family moved back up to Kansas.

So he'd always think of the Kansas town of Abilene as his real home. Just about twenty miles from the exact middle of the whole country, Abilene was not very different from hundreds of other American towns in the horse-and-buggy days near the end of the 1800s. If his parents had aimed to choose a typically peaceful and hard-working community for bringing up their sons, they couldn't have done better.

Actually, David and Ida Eisenhower had been most influenced by the fact that many of their relatives had already settled in this area during the past ten or fifteen years. David's father and grandfather had left Pennsylvania to join a religious group planning a new colony on fertile Kansas farmland. And David's future wife, when she'd been Ida Stover, had departed from Virginia with a similar group.

Besides being deeply religious, Ida Stover had an unusual notion for a girl in those days. She wanted to go to college, and she'd managed to enroll at a small one called Lane, in the Kansas town of Lecompton. There she met a young man as shy as she was talkative. His hair and eyes were dark, and he took life seriously. Her hair was so light that it seemed white in the sunlight, and her eyes were sparkling blue. For even though she held some serious opinions, she was so naturally cheerful that she could no more keep from smiling than the sun could keep from shining.

Despite all their differences, David and Ida soon found that they were more alike than most people would guess. Both could trace their families back to solid farmers who'd come to America in the 1700s from Germany or

Switzerland. Both were members of a high-minded religious sect called the River Brethren. By the end of their second year at Lane, they also agreed that they had gained whatever they could from this far-from-elaborate learning center with just a few classrooms. In September of 1885, in the Kansas village of Hope, they were married.

Their first two sons—Arthur and Edgar—were born above the general store the young husband opened there with a partner. For David Eisenhower had a stubborn streak. The only aspect of farming that had appealed to him during his boyhood was tinkering with machines, so he'd wanted to study engineering. Now that was impossible, but he still would not accept his father's plan and become a farmer after all. Instead he sold the land he got as a wedding present, then put the profit into this business venture.

However, the store failed. It was his partner's fault, Ida Eisenhower would always insist. But she also said she didn't believe in crying over spilled milk, so she briskly set about proving she could raise a large family without worrying about money.

Her third son, Dwight, was eight months old when they moved to Abilene, where his father began working at a plant that bottled cream from local farms. David Eisenhower's pay for tending the machinery was just forty dollars a month—and it never went much higher.

While prices were a good deal lower then (eggs sold for five cents a dozen), Dwight's mother still performed something like a miracle.

By the time Dwight was ten years old he had five brothers, and they were all sturdy youngsters. To buy enough food for them would have cost more than their father earned—but fortunately their trim white cottage sat on two acres. The property also had a roomy barn. So in addition to growing bushels of fruit and vegetables, they milked their own cows and raised chickens and pigs, too.

"They" were the Eisenhower boys. For as soon as one of her sons could carry an armful of kindling, Mrs. Eisenhower saw to it that he did his share of chores, indoors and out. They took turns at the different jobs, from toting steaming buckets of laundry water to picking strawberries. There was no escaping, either, unless they wanted a whipping.

But even though both their parents would swiftly punish any offender, the boys rarely felt mistreated. Once they'd done their chores, they knew, they were free to play ball or go fishing. Of course, sometimes they got to fighting—especially Dwight. For it wasn't hard to get his dander up.

Once when he was ten, he lost his temper spectacularly, and that led to what he later recalled as one of the most valuable moments of his life.

When Dwight's fifth grade posed for its class picture, he was the only boy wearing overalls because his family couldn't afford finer clothes. He's second from the left in the front row.

It was on Halloween, and his parents said his two older brothers could go out trick-or-treating after supper. Dwight longed to go with them, but he was told he was too young. That made him furious. When Art and Ed departed, his rage reached such a pitch that, not even knowing how it happened, he found himself outside pounding his fists at the trunk of an apple tree.

He must have been bellowing at the top of his lungs, too, because his father suddenly grabbed him and shook him by the shoulders. Only then did Dwight notice that his own fists were cut and bleeding. To his father, such a display of temper demanded strong action, so he immediately smacked his son's bottom severely. Then he decreed, "Young man, to bed!"

About half an hour later, Dwight's mother quietly slipped into the boy's room and sat down in a rocking chair. He was still sobbing bitterly into his pillow, and after a few minutes Mrs. Eisenhower began talking about temper and about controlling it.

Getting so angry at anyone or anything was useless, she said, because you couldn't hurt anybody but yourself that way. While she went on telling him how much harm he could cause himself by letting his temper control his actions, she was gently washing his hands with a cloth and then applying soothing ointment. As she was wrapping some bandage around the worst places, she put her lesson into the language of the Bible:

"He that conquereth his own soul is greater than he who taketh a city."

Then Dwight found it possible to say he was sorry, and soon he felt calm enough to fall asleep. After that, when he got angry he tried his best to keep from showing it.

2 TAKING TURNS

Of course, Dwight got into plenty of scrapes and fights, which he usually won—except when he was battling his brother Ed, who was not only older but also bigger. Their constant roughing around didn't fool anyone, though. Even their mother realized they were just having fun.

Dwight had great fun, in fact, during the years he went to grade school and high school. It didn't bother him a bit that they lived on the wrong side of the railroad tracks and that he never had any spending money unless he worked for it. He really enjoyed the challenge of thinking up new ways to earn whatever he needed.

For instance, when he wanted a baseball mitt one spring, he had a brainstorm. He always looked forward to his turn at cooking Sunday dinner, and he could produce a pretty good meal, from vegetable soup to apple pie. So he asked his mother to teach him a Mexican specialty she'd learned in Texas. Then he sold hot tamales, three for a nickel, until he'd saved enough to buy the glove he craved.

Dwight and Ed, being not much more than a year apart, naturally did most of their working and playing as a team. Toward the end of summer, when their interest shifted toward football, they'd fill a wagon with surplus corn and cucumbers, hitch up a horse, then go peddling their vegetables across the tracks at the back doors of the big houses there. With their profits they'd buy helmets, or maybe powder and shot for the ancient muzzle-loading guns they had got when they were old enough to go hunting.

As they grew bigger, they also hired out to do odd jobs like apple picking. And instead of just going fishing on the Smoky Hill River with Old Bob Davis, they'd take some lessons from him—in the fine points of a particular card game.

After dealing out five cards, Old Bob would ask Dwight whether he held any pair in his hand.

"Yes, nines."

"All right," Bob would say, "how many nines are there out of the forty-seven cards that you have not yet seen?"

Of course, the answer was two.

"Well, then," Bob would go on, "the chance of your drawing a nine as you take the next card is two out of forty-seven, and since you will be drawing three cards, you'll have six chances out of forty-seven of catching a third nine."

So by the time Dwight was a high school senior, he was quite an expert at the game of poker. He knew all about percentages—far more than he'd learned in his math classes. Except for math and history, he didn't care much about his marks, and even in those subjects he scored as little more than an average student. Nevertheless he stood out, for other reasons.

Besides being intensely fond of sports, he was pretty good at football and baseball and he rarely got beaten in boxing matches or running races. It wasn't just because of all this, though, that he was elected president of the Abilene High School Athletic Association. It was also because everybody liked him—"Ike" Eisenhower was one of the most popular young fellows in town.

How did the nickname start? He never could figure that out, nor did he see why it stuck. But he'd long since got used to being called Ike, even if, privately, he preferred his real name. Anyway, he had more important matters to think about, with graduation approaching.

At the ceremonies, the main speaker was a newspaper editor from the state capital who was supposed to be a good bet for the next governor. Something he said made a deep impression on Dwight.

Dwight, in the foreground, on a camping trip with some of his friends while he was in high school.

"I would sooner begin life over again with one arm cut off than attempt to struggle along without a college education," this man declared.

Until then, Dwight hadn't been sure if he wanted to try for college. Part of the time he felt he ought to, because he had some grand ideas about his future hidden under his easygoing manner. George Washington was his hero, and he was pretty certain he wouldn't be satisfied spending his life in a routine job.

What's more, both his parents wanted the best possible education for their boys—they'd been disappointed when Arthur, the eldest, had gone off to work in a Kansas City bank without any advanced schooling. It was understood that each boy would have to earn his own way, but Dwight didn't hesitate because of that. His problem was that he felt perfectly happy at this point just enjoying himself in Abilene.

After he and Ed listened to that speaker, however, they arrived at an unusual plan. They decided to take turns attending college. While one of them studied, the other would get a job and send most of his earnings to support his student brother. Then in two years they'd change places—at least that's what they expected to do.

Since Ed was eager to start carrying out his personal program of becoming a lawyer, he left home first. He went to the University of Michigan, which was highly regarded in the legal field.

Meanwhile Dwight began lifting and carrying milk cans at the creamery where his father still tended the machinery. If David Eisenhower had any ideas about this son's future, he didn't mention them. When his own father had tried to force him into farming, he'd vowed he would let any children he might have choose their course by themselves. He hadn't made the slightest attempt to influence either of Dwight's elder brothers, and now he followed the same policy again.

But within a year, David and Ida Eisenhower were both sorely tempted to speak out. For Dwight told them a new plan that made his eyes glint with excitement. He had learned of a way to get a fine education at no cost: at West Point, where the federal government trained officers for the United States Army.

So it didn't matter that he'd had no clear notion of what he wanted to be. Suddenly he could see all sorts of opportunities opening up for him, if he became a soldier. Yet he couldn't help knowing how unhappy this career would make his parents because of their religious beliefs. To them all wars were evil, and it would hurt them just to see one of their sons wearing a soldier's uniform. To soften his blow, Dwight assured them he'd undoubtedly fail the West Point entrance exams.

But after studying every spare moment for another year, he passed. Still he wondered whether he ought to go ahead with a step that would cause his mother so much pain.

"It's your decision," she said gently. And Dwight pondered the matter for months, until he decided that he could not pass up such a wonderful chance.

Then he wrote to accept the place that had been offered to him, and on a warm June morning in 1911, when he was approaching his twenty-first birthday, he came downstairs carrying a suitcase. His mother was waiting on the front porch. Her eyes were dry as she kissed him goodbye. She even tried to smile, leading Dwight to promise himself that someday he'd make her proud of him after all.

3 BEAST BARRACKS

"Get your chin back!"

"Hold your head up!"

"Get your shoulders back!"

"Keep running double time, mister!"

Cadet Eisenhower thought he might be the clumsiest oaf who'd ever entered West Point. During his first few days there he felt totally confused by the rapid fire of orders from superior upperclassmen. His feet, in particular, refused to do his bidding.

"Get in step!" the drill instructors shouted.

But he couldn't seem to keep to the beat of the marching band—and so he was assigned to the Awkward Squad.

Very soon, though, Dwight was doing better. It even struck him that he was really much better prepared for all this strictness than most of his fellow plebes. He was accustomed to constant exercise, and he hadn't been pampered at home. Besides, he was nearly twenty-one, which made him a wise old man in the Beast Barracks, as the big stone dorm for new arrivals was called.

His own roommate, for instance, was barely seventeen —a brainy kid just out of high school who had been treated like a hero when he won admission to the famous military academy. Everybody in town had come to see him off, and the mayor had made a speech. Then suddenly here he was, being barked at constantly. He just couldn't take it.

Dwight tried to tell him that the point of all this drilling and hollering wasn't merely to torture them. An assorted bunch of freewheeling fellows had to be taught a different attitude pretty quickly: if you were a soldier, you had to follow orders. Once you learned the basic lesson, the barking would let up.

But Dwight's roommate didn't want to hear about how many thousands of boys had gone through the same experience and survived. "Where else could you get a college education without cost?" Dwight asked him. That didn't work either. Practically every night, the roommate put his head down while he was supposedly studying and wept into his hands.

So Dwight wasn't surprised when this poor fellow didn't return from their first furlough at Christmas. About 50 others of the 285 in their class also dropped

Cadet Eisenhower, at the left, on guard duty at West Point.

out. Although Cadet Eisenhower had already got more than his share of demerits (for such faults as not having his hat on straight), he didn't even consider quitting.

Ever since he'd managed to pass the entrance exams by boning up on his own, he'd felt plenty of self-confidence where books were concerned. Thus he didn't worry about flunking any course—nor did he care about getting top marks. What he did care about was sports.

More than anything else, he yearned to make the football team.

By spending every spare minute out practicing, he developed a lot of speed. By cramming in mammoth meals, he put on 20 pounds, bringing his weight up to 174. That was still pretty light for varsity playing, but at least it was solid muscle, evenly distributed along his sturdy five feet eleven inches. His main asset, though, was his fierce desire to gain ground whenever he got hold of the ball.

As a result, the coach began using him as a plunging back during his sophomore year. With two more years ahead of him, Dwight foresaw quite a career. He loved the game, and the idea of being a star on the Army team —why, nothing in the world could beat that!

Then came the next to last game of his sophomore season.

They were playing against Tufts. Cadet Eisenhower plunged through the Tufts line for a fair gain, but as he was going through, one of the opposing linemen grabbed his foot. Pushing to get a few extra yards, Dwight threw his whole weight and power forward, twisting his own leg. He heard and felt something rip, although it didn't hurt particularly. He picked himself up for the next play, ran a few steps, and fell. He couldn't get up.

Two days later, Dwight's knee seemed back to normal and he was released from the infirmary. He was hoping the coach would let him play in the final game against Navy after all. But within the week, while he was taking part in a regular horseback riding drill, he jumped to the ground and the shock severely jolted the same knee. This time the doctors shook their heads and pronounced a terrible verdict.

No more rugged sports for Cadet Eisenhower. Ever.

Then Dwight really started suffering. His spirits sank so low that his friends were alarmed. Somehow he'd become known at West Point, too, as Ike—and for the rest of that year dozens of other cadets did their best to keep Ike from dropping out of the academy. Several times he actually signed the papers resigning his place, but each time his classmates convinced him to tear them up.

In various efforts to show him he could still help Army teams win, they chose Ike as a cheerleader or a manager. Yet he still felt hopelessly sidelined. If he couldn't be on the field carrying the ball, why bother obeying the rules?

During those dismal months he took to smoking ciga-rettes where he was bound to be caught, and he didn't mind how many punishment tours he had to walk.

Nevertheless Ike's natural cheerfulness couldn't be kept down indefinitely. Eventually, he got interested in strengthening his arm and shoulder muscles by working out on rowing machines. And while he didn't know any girls he especially liked, he went to a few dances. Most weekends when a hop was scheduled, though, he stayed at the dorm playing poker, and his early training back in Kansas made him a big winner.

Even so, he was easily one of the most popular mem-bers of the Class of 1915. By the time graduation rolled around, this class, like most others, had lost more than one third of its original strength. Despite having ignored a lot of rules, Cadet Dwight Eisenhower was still on the roster, but his record showed that in matters of discipline only 47 of the remaining 162 men had done worse than he had. As far as his exam marks were concerned he came out somewhat better, ranking 61st from the top. It wasn't exactly a distinguished standing, but he'd safely passed and would soon be an officer in the United States Army. Along with the other graduates, he'd receive the gold bar of a second lieutenant.

Or would he?

During his last weeks at West Point, Cadet Eisen-hower was summoned by the chief medical officer, who raised the question of his injured knee. Although he'd been forced to spend a few days in the post hospital every so often when the knee got strained, nobody had ever suggested that this cadet might not be physically fit for Army service. Now the doctor calmly suggested it.

Dwight had really enjoyed West Point, no matter how much he griped sometimes. He also felt he owed his country a lot for the past four years. Beneath his carefree manner he was stirred by ambitions to excel, and he soberly believed he'd make a good officer.

Yet he also had a streak of the rebel in him. "Well, I don't care too much," he told the doctor. "I'll just take my savings"—he paused to think a second, then grinned—"and I'll go to Argentina."

The doctor looked startled, and Dwight was amazed himself. While he'd always been curious about the Argentine, the notion of going there had just popped into his head.

"Let me think this over," the doctor said.

Dwight didn't have much hope, though, and that evening he did write away for some travel folders about South America. He was fully expecting a final rebuff when he was called back to the medical office a few days later. But the doctor started out by noting that riding on a horse aggravated the knee injury.

"Mr. Eisenhower," he said, "if you will not ask for a

mounted service, I will recommend you for a commission."

Dwight had always liked horses, and the cavalry was one of the main branches of the Army then. But he did not hesitate.

"That's all right with me," he said. "I want to go in the infantry, anyway."

So he filled out a form stating that he'd prefer foot soldiery, and that he'd like to be assigned to serve with the American forces stationed at the country's Pacific outpost in the Philippine Islands.

Of course the Army had its own ideas on that matter. Second Lieutenant Dwight Eisenhower's first orders were to report for duty at Fort Sam Houston, near San Antonio, Texas.

4 MISSING THE BOAT

There were two reasons why Fort Sam Houston appealed to young Army officers in 1915. For the past several years, United States relations with nearby Mexico had been growing increasingly tense. So the men at this post might soon have the excitement of real fighting, instead of just training exercises. Yet if they preferred escorting pretty girls to parties, they also had plenty of opportunities because San Antonio had a large number of well-off families who liked to entertain lieutenants.

Second Lieutenant Eisenhower didn't think he'd have much fun at fancy dances. But one Sunday afternoon in October, while he was on guard duty, the wife of a major walked up to him with a small group of visitors.

"Ike," she said, "I have some people I'd like you to meet."

Their name was Doud. They came from Denver, and they spent the winter months every year in this sunny climate. Or so Ike gathered later—for at this first meeting his whole attention was captured by these people's daughter.

She looked saucy, he decided. Smaller than average, with lively eyes and with the pertest smile he'd ever seen. On an impulse he asked her to walk around the post with him, and to his happy surprise she agreed. From then on, he devoted every spare minute to trying to win the heart of Mamie Doud.

Until then, Ike had rather relished his reputation of being a woman-hater. But suddenly he found himself unmistakably in love, and he faced quite a challenge. Except for his Army pay, amounting to just $141.67 a month, he had no money with which to take Mamie out to expensive restaurants—and she was accustomed to the best of everything. What's more, a lot of other young men kept bringing her bouquets of flowers or otherwise seeking to impress her.

As a suitor, though, Ike had a great advantage he didn't even imagine. In his own mind, if he ever gave the matter any thought, he barely escaped being homely, but actually his picture could have been used on a recruiting poster. With his reddish hair and intensely blue eyes, his wholesome, outdoor air, and his tall, sturdy frame set off by his uniform, he immediately inspired friendly feelings. When something amused him, as happened very often, he became more than merely handsome. Ike's grin was very hard to resist.

Mamie could not resist it. Despite her usually finicky tastes she cheerfully accompanied him to far-from-elegant eateries where two could dine on Mexican chili for one dollar, including tip. They attended the Orpheum's vaudeville show, sitting in the cheapest seats. On Valentine's Day, barely four months after they'd met, she let him give her his class ring, and they were officially engaged.

Although Mamie's parents must have expected this news, they urged the young couple to delay making any marriage plans. Not that Mr. and Mrs. Doud didn't like Ike—along with practically everybody else who knew him, they liked him enormously. But Mamie was only nineteen, and they thought she should wait at least a year before marrying.

However, world events now had a decisive effect on Second Lieutenant Eisenhower's wedding arrangements. Besides the Mexican troubles, which were still seething, the great war that had erupted in Europe in 1914 was reaching a new pitch of ferocity. It seemed more and more likely that the United States would become involved. Mamie was terrified that Ike might be shipped off to fight in some foreign land—but if he had to go, she was determined to be his wife before he departed.

So the wedding took place on July 1, 1916, at the Presbyterian church in Denver where the Douds worshipped. The ceremony was arranged on such short notice, right after the lieutenant received a ten-day leave, that none of his own family could be present. But en route back to San Antonio, the twenty-five-year-old Ike and his bride stopped briefly in Abilene to see his relatives. Ike's mother welcomed her daughter-in-law with a wonderful fried chicken banquet for breakfast.

Despite their long and tiring train ride, the newlyweds were thrilled to find a party greeting them when they reached Fort Sam Houston. There hadn't been time to send out any formal wedding announcements, yet somehow the word had spread. Ike's tiny bachelor apartment was packed with gift packages, most of them containing cooking equipment such as a toaster, a broiler, a coffee pot.

Considering the uncertainty of his future, Ike hadn't expected that they would set up housekeeping. The officers' mess was directly across the street, and he thought they'd eat there since wives were allowed to do so. Yet he hadn't bargained on his young bride's willpower.

Even though she knew less about cooking than he did, she knew what she didn't like—and cold mashed potatoes came near the top of her list. Since this unpleasant item was a staple on the menu of the mess, Mamie vowed to provide better meals herself. Soon she was preparing such good dinners that they could sometimes invite a few friends to join them.

Dwight and Mamie on their wedding day, July 1, 1916.

For no new orders turned up after all. Month after month, while the threat of war came ever closer, rumors about transfers kept spreading, but the only change in Ike's status was a promotion to first lieutenant. Yet his duties, involving the training of new recruits, remained basically the same, except that he was also assigned to spend part of his time coaching a soldiers' football team.

This pleased Mamie, of course. When the United States did declare war on Germany, after American ships had been sunk by German submarines, the young Mrs. Eisenhower was expecting a baby. So she couldn't help hoping her husband would stay with her—and he did. Their son, David, was born on September 24, 1917.

Although Ike was elated to become a father, and he hated the idea of being separated from Mamie, he still felt terribly restless. Before getting married he'd applied to join a new branch of the service that was teaching soldiers to fly airplanes, but Mamie's parents had objected. They didn't think he should seek such a dangerous assignment.

He'd let them convince him then, but now the country was at war. By going to West Point he'd committed himself to becoming an Army officer instead of taking up some other profession. Now men without his special skills were risking their lives under enemy fire. How could he just keep on doing safe and routine duty?

Besides, he still felt the need to excel that had made

him long to be a football star. Staying on the sidelines could never satisfy him. Since any army's basic purpose was to win wars, its leaders had to have battle experience, and many of his own classmates were already making names for themselves overseas in France. From their ranks would come the future generals of the United States Army—and Ike couldn't help secretly seeing himself wearing the star of a general on his uniform someday.

So he pulled every string he could to get sent overseas. But every time he applied for a transfer he was swiftly turned down. Once he was even warned that his record would show he'd disobeyed his superiors if he didn't stop making these requests.

He was doing a fine job right where he was, the senior officers assured him. In their eyes, Ike was clearly a very likable but not a very talented young man. They appeared to believe that he wasn't capable of tackling any more challenging task than supervising the training of raw recruits.

Yet as the pace of American military operations speeded up, First Lieutenant Eisenhower inevitably was given some new responsibilities.

Instead of just training recruits, he got the job of organizing whole new units. To the pleased surprise of his superiors, he turned out to be a splendid organizer. He also showed a real gift for cutting through red tape to secure necessary supplies. Soon he got a temporary rank of captain, then of major, and then lieutenant colonel. Under the pressure of wartime expansion, temporary promotions like these were fairly common among West Point graduates.

Finally, in October of 1918, Lieutenant Colonel Eisenhower got the orders he'd been longing for so eagerly. By now he was commanding officer of Camp Colt in Pennsylvania, where he had charge of training a new category of troops: soldiers who did their fighting aboard the new kind of heavily armored vehicles called tanks. For the past seven months he'd been entrusted with the task of taking in several thousand volunteers every month, equipping and instructing them, then getting them embarked on ships sailing for France. But not until October was he told that he'd be allowed to accompany the next contingent, due to sail around the middle of November.

However, the news from Europe suddenly changed. German resistance weakened all along the fighting front, and on November 11, joyful bells clanged the message that an armistice had been signed. The war was over!

Ike had missed the boat, as he wryly put it. All further troop shipments were of course canceled. And, in the words of President Wilson, this had been a war to end all wars forever. Therefore, as far as Dwight Eisenhower could see, his personal future looked rather unappealing.

"I saw myself in the years ahead putting on weight in a meaningless chair-bound assignment, shuffling papers and filling out forms," he wrote much later. As a result, he seriously considered resigning from the Army and trying his luck at a new career.

5 FIRST AT LAST

Ike was twenty-eight years old in 1918, and he had a wife and son to support. If he stayed in the Army, his pay as even a lieutenant colonel wouldn't buy many luxuries. But temporary promotions would surely be wiped off the books soon. He'd be bumped down to captain then, which meant that he and Mamie would really have to count their pennies.

Furthermore, in the peacetime Army promotions came very slowly. It might be fifteen years until he got back up to lieutenant colonel—assuming he'd go that far. With a lot of luck he might become a full colonel before retiring, although his chances for a general's star had just about disappeared.

So Ike was tempted to accept a job that he was offered by an Indiana businessman who'd been on his staff at Camp Colt during the final months of the war. The pay was better than he could possibly expect in the Army.

Yet did he really want to spend the rest of his life helping to run a factory?

No! Ike had scores of friends from West Point and the various posts where he'd served. He'd sorely miss the comradeship of Army life, and he felt comfortable with the Army's traditions. He even thought he might find some way to do more than merely mark time if he stayed in uniform.

At Camp Meade in Maryland, where he was sent shortly after the fighting stopped, he made one discovery within a few months. He still loved to play poker, and with the pressures of the war emergency now relaxed he'd take a hand whenever he stopped at the officers' club. And he won regularly because he calculated the odds before he picked any card, instead of getting carried away by emotion the way many of his opponents did. As a result, some other players lost more than they could afford.

One morning, Captain Eisenhower was approached by a man who'd lost heavily the night before. Could the debt be paid, he asked, with government bonds?

"Okay," Ike said, but he suddenly felt miserable, knowing that those bonds had been bought with the money the man's wife had scrimped to save for the children they might have. How could Ike give the money back without insulting the young officer? The solution he thought of was rather complicated.

The next evening another poker game was organized—and all the other players had secretly promised to let the heavy loser win. But it wasn't easy. Ike had such a run of lucky cards that he had to do ridiculous things like dropping an ace on the floor, supposedly by accident. Around midnight the deed finally was done, and Ike had made himself a private promise: never again would he play poker with Army buddies.

However, living quarters for officers' families became available soon afterward, so Ike now had his family to keep him from getting bored. He'd had only brief visits with Mamie and their son since he'd left San Antonio, and even though the barracks apartment they were now assigned was rather primitive, they were delighted to be together again.

Exactly how it happened that their boy had come to be called "Icky" by practically everybody was something his parents couldn't quite explain—but nobody could help loving Icky. At the age of three, he was a happy little fellow who quickly became the pet of the whole post.

When his father let him climb aboard a tank, Icky looked as if nothing in the world could be more fun. But "helping" to coach the football team made his eyes glow even brighter, and if he got to watch a parade of soldiers stepping smartly in time to the music of the marching band, his joy overflowed into the most excited chortling of all.

Because Icky was such a lively child, his parents felt he had to be watched every minute. So they hired a girl who lived in the area to mind him while his mother did other necessary chores. The girl seemed perfectly healthy —nobody told them she'd been sick recently with a mild case of a disease that could be extremely severe.

It was scarlet fever. Only after Icky became ill did the camp's doctors decide that the girl must still have carried enough of the infection to make her a menace. For Icky's case was dreadfully serious. Although specialists were summoned from the outstanding hospital in nearby Baltimore, there was no known medicine then to combat the acute attack, which gradually sapped the strength of the sturdy little boy. Day by day he got weaker, and on the second day of the sad new year of 1921, he died.

Nearly fifty years later, his father would write, "I have never known such a blow."

For both parents, the year after the death of their first-born son was the hardest they would ever face. Yet somehow they both slowly emerged from their numbing grief. This healing process owed much to one of Captain Eisenhower's fellow officers—a major who was already famous, at least in the Army.

His name was George Patton, and his fame stemmed from his flamboyant exploits over in France. As the leader of one of the first battalions of tanks ever to face an enemy, he had dashed about with such disregard for his own safety that he'd cut through the German lines an incredible number of times. Despite his swaggering manner, though, Major Patton also liked to study military tactics.

Soon he and Ike were spending their spare hours making field tests of various sizes of tanks. They even got a mechanic to put together an experimental model that could be maneuvered more easily than the cumbersome monsters that had been used in France. For Ike had some theories about how tanks might be adapted to perform many different functions, thereby opening a new chapter in warfare. Thanks to George Patton, he was able to distract his mind during the terrible months after his son's death by getting more and more involved with research regarding tanks.

Then Ike's friend did him another service, which would prove to be the turning point of his career. Patton invited him to dinner when Brigadier General Fox Conner was visiting the post.

General Conner, who'd been one of General Pershing's chief aides during the World War, was leaving shortly for a new assignment near the Panama Canal. He was very much impressed by Eisenhower's ideas about tanks, and he arranged to have Ike transferred to his own staff. During the next three years, Ike really used his head for the first time in his life.

For it turned out that General Conner was a great

teacher. Sensing that his new aide had some hidden talents, the general asked him a casual question one evening. Ike grinned and replied that he really wasn't too interested in military history ever since he'd had to memorize so many dull details at West Point.

General Conner made no comment, but soon Ike was invited to the general's quarters, where he couldn't avoid noticing how many books were on the shelves. "You might be interested in these," Conner remarked, picking out a few fast-paced action stories that took place during various wars.

Ike read these stories and enjoyed them. When he returned the books, the general asked him what he thought of them, and they talked awhile about the stories. "Wouldn't you like to know something of what the armies were actually doing during the periods of these novels?" General Conner asked.

Then Ike thought maybe he would—and soon he was intently reading more serious books on military subjects. Each time he returned a book, he and the general talked about it. Ike found himself becoming very interested in analyzing military campaigns of the past.

Being a man of broad learning, the general next introduced his pupil to many famous authors in different fields. Ike was astonished to find how fascinating some of those ancient Romans were, and Shakespeare, and various French writers he'd never heard of before. So he learned more in his three years in Panama than he'd learned all the rest of his life.

Something even more exciting happened while he was stationed there. Mamie gave birth to a husky boy, whom they named John, and the private grief they still felt was overshadowed by a new surge of happiness.

But after three years in such a steamy climate, they were glad to hear a rumor that new orders were imminent. When these assigned him back to Camp Meade for more troop training and football coaching, Ike felt awfully disappointed. Yet something better was in store for him—so much better that Major Eisenhower had to worry about whether he could handle the new assignment.

It was to attend the Army's Command and General Staff School at Fort Leavenworth in Kansas. Only officers who had demonstrated exceptional ability were admitted there, and most of the students had much broader experience than Ike had managed to get since leaving West Point. In a letter to General Conner, who'd undoubtedly had much to do with getting him into such a highly regarded program, Ike pointed out that he would be competing against men who'd already passed a rigorous course at another Army training center.

"You will feel no sense of inferiority," General Conner wrote back.

Even so, Ike did some studying on his own before he

Major Eisenhower at a family reunion in Abilene in 1926.

reported to Fort Leavenworth in the spring of 1925. There he put in a tough year of attending classes and tackling complicated problems that defeated many of his fellow students.

When the year ended, Eisenhower had the great satisfaction of being recorded the top man among the 275 graduates. So he was first at last.

6 IN THE WINGS

With such an outstanding achievement to his credit, Major Eisenhower moved into a new category of the Army after he left Fort Leavenworth. For his name went down on a special list kept locked up in Washington. This was a list of military officers who had demonstrated superior ability and from whose ranks would come the Army's future generals—if ever another war involved the United States.

But unless the uniformed services had to expand under the pressure of some unforeseen emergency, Ike's chances for advancement were still very limited. The nation's political leaders knew that military spending was extremely unpopular during peacetime, so they routinely cut military budgets to the bare minimum. The whole Army in 1926 contained fewer than 200,000 men, compared with nearly 5 million at the peak of the World War a few years earlier. Promotions for officers came strictly by seniority, and the members of Major Eisenhower's

West Point class wouldn't even make lieutenant colonel until another ten years passed.

By now, Ike accepted this as the way things were, and besides he was pretty contented with his personal income level. Even if he'd never be rich, he and Mamie and their son were really living quite comfortably on a salary that might seem small by civilian standards. The Army provided many free services, such as medical treatment, making it easier for them to manage. In addition, he had plenty of golf partners for his spare hours, and Mamie had plenty of parties at which she could smilingly improvise all sorts of tunes on the piano while everybody stood around singing.

In short, Ike had no serious complaints—except in one department. Especially after he'd done well at Leavenworth, couldn't the Army find a better job for him than just another round of routine training plus football coaching?

That's what his next assignment was, this time at Fort Benning in Georgia. Yet the high brass in Washington weren't as blind as some people thought. Even though the United States Army offered few opportunities in the late 1920s, Ike did receive more stimulating tasks as the years passed. When Congress authorized the compiling of a history of America's military role during the World War, Eisenhower finally got to Europe and spent many months carefully touring the former battlefields. Then he was tapped to attend the Army's most advanced training school for staff officers. At the beginning of the 1930s, he had his first taste of the political side of military activities when he became an aide to the Assistant Secretary of War in President Hoover's Cabinet. In Washington he also helped old General Pershing compile his memoirs.

While none of these assignments brought Major Eisenhower the slightest notice in any newspaper, his more than merely capable performance of such varied duties did reward him with added attention from the upper ranks of the Army itself. Beyond question the most colorful figure among the country's military leaders then was General Douglas MacArthur, who made Ike his chief aide in 1933.

A good many officers would have hated this job, but Ike relished it. Although MacArthur was tremendously impressed with his own importance and behaved, even in private, like a ham actor strutting across a stage, such mannerisms amused his new aide instead of upsetting him. Ike sensed that underneath all these oddities was a keen mind with an awesome knowledge of military science.

Without question, MacArthur had a wider range of Army experience than any other man alive. As the son of a general who had played a leading part in winning the Philippine Islands in 1898, Douglas MacArthur had grown up on Army posts, then gone on to surpass his father's own career. After displaying amazing bravery in the World War, he'd been put in charge of modernizing

West Point and had commanded the country's Far Eastern forces stationed in the Philippines. Now he held the top Army position as Chief of Staff.

For two years, Ike sat in the next office to this remarkable man, drafting reports and letters that MacArthur usually signed with a bold flourish. By and large, the excitable general and his cheerfully competent assistant got along well together. Often, though, Ike would have to gulp to keep from laughing, for MacArthur had a habit that struck him as enormously comical. The general spoke of himself as if he were discussing another person. "MacArthur has had a very trying day," he would say, or, "MacArthur is distressed by the tone of this newspaper article." Ike sometimes was sorely tempted to ask who this fellow was that his boss was always describing.

But Ike's main gripe was about Washington itself. He'd never particularly liked the place because its only industry was politics, a subject that irritated him under normal circumstances. If he possibly could, he stayed clear of all political talk. In 1933, though, it was awfully hard to steer away from such topics, for the times were far from normal.

Ever since 1929, economic conditions around the country had been getting worse and worse. With no sign of improvement in sight, the American people had taken a chance and chosen Franklin D. Roosevelt as their President. At least Ike thought they were taking quite a risk, although he never said so publicly.

Roosevelt's New Deal politics couldn't help but disturb a conservative-minded Army officer. Ike didn't think of himself as carrying any political label, and only his closest friends knew his opinions, but as FDR kept pumping more millions of the taxpayers' money into all sorts of programs that were supposed to bring back prosperity, Ike became increasingly restless in the nation's capital.

So he was relieved and pleased when in 1935 MacArthur's tour of duty as Chief of Staff ended, and he himself was asked to accompany the general to the Philippines. Congress had recently passed a measure granting the islands independence in ten more years, meanwhile authorizing various steps to help the Philippine people prepare for self-government. It would be Eisenhower's mission to advise the islanders on setting up their own armed force, capable of taking over protective duties after the American flag no longer flew above Manila.

Almost immediately upon arriving in that Far Eastern city, Ike realized that his task was nearly hopeless. Neither the American Congress nor the new Philippine legislature was willing to provide the funds for more than a tiny token force. General MacArthur simply would not face the reality of this financial lack, and friction between the two men became an increasing problem in the next four years.

Even so, Ike wasn't exactly unhappy in Manila. One

Lieutenant Colonel Eisenhower, at the left, with two of his fellow officers in the Philippines.

reason was that his promotion to lieutenant colonel finally came through. Furthermore, he and Mamie enjoyed the luxury of living in an air-conditioned hotel suite and being treated as very important persons by Philippine officials. Yet, by 1939, he could hardly wait to get back to the States.

For another great war was coming—he felt sure of it. From the vantage point of the Far East, no experienced military man could doubt that Japan would sooner or later provoke a conflict with the United States. Already the Japanese leaders had sent troops into China, and the expansionist policies of that island empire seemed bound to pose a growing threat to American interests.

But Ike thought the threat in Europe was even more dangerous. Because the German people had let a madman named Hitler take over their government, the peace won in 1918 couldn't possibly last much longer. The small countries of Austria and Czechoslovakia had already been seized by Nazi German forces, and Hitler made no secret of his schemes for further conquest. Although England and France had pledged to stop him, could they do it alone? No, Ike grimly thought, the United States would surely be involved too.

And when that happened, this time he wouldn't stay on the sidelines!

So, in September of 1939—right after World War II erupted over in Europe—Lieutenant Colonel Dwight

Eisenhower appealed to Washington for an immediate transfer. He didn't want another desk job. To prepare himself for leading troops into combat, he wanted some field experience as commander of a brigade of foot soldiers.

But some of the high officers who had been keeping him in mind had a different idea. They wanted Ike assigned to the war planning staff in Washington, where they thought he could serve his country best. However, a sort of compromise was arranged after Ike told his friends how much he longed for active duty now.

His new assignment did have to do with planning, although not at Army headquarters in the nation's capital. Instead he was attached to the group of soldiers described on the War Department's charts as the United States Third Army. Ike's first responsibility was to plan the most extensive training maneuvers ever undertaken by United States troops.

Then he spent months in the sticky heat of Louisiana observing the strong points and the weak points of his combat plans. His tent became a focal point where everybody from junior officers to journalists came to find out what was supposed to be happening in the fake contests being fought all over the sparsely settled area. Of course, real bullets could not be used, so a lot of play-acting had to be done. This situation gave rise to numerous stories, among which was Eisenhower's own favorite:

An umpire decided that a bridge had been destroyed by an "enemy" attack and flagged it accordingly. From then on, it was not to be used by men or vehicles. Shortly, a corporal brought his squad up to the bridge, looked at the flag, and hesitated a moment. Then he resolutely marched his men across. The umpire yelled at him:

"Hey, don't you see that that bridge is destroyed?"

The corporal answered: "Of course I can see it's destroyed. Can't you see we're swimming?"

But despite the game-playing attitude that produced this kind of humor, the top brass must have thought that the Louisiana maneuvers actually served a very useful purpose, because soon after they ended Dwight Eisenhower received some surprising news. He'd been "jumped" over dozens of colonels who were ahead of him in seniority—he'd been awarded a star.

So it was Brigadier General Dwight Eisenhower who told his orderly after lunch on Sunday, December 7, 1941, that he felt awfully tired and was going back to his quarters for a nap. Under no circumstances did he want to be wakened, General Eisenhower said.

But the orderly used his own judgment.

An hour later, he woke the general to tell him that the Japanese had just attacked Pearl Harbor.

Colonel Eisenhower relaxing in his tent during Army maneuvers in Louisiana in 1941.

7 "HOP A PLANE!"

The next several days were among the hardest Ike Eisenhower had ever spent.

Along with millions of his fellow Americans, he heard the solemn voice of President Roosevelt over the radio on December 8, addressing an emergency session of Congress. Then the nation's lawmakers declared war against Japan. Germany and Italy, having previously joined Japan in an "Axis," or alliance, proclaimed that they, too, were now at war with the United States. Congress acted again, officially bringing the country into the conflict in Europe.

So by December 11, the United States had gone through all the formal steps involved in entering the greatest war in history—and Dwight Eisenhower was still waiting impatiently for new orders to reach him at his Texas headquarters.

Finally, early the next morning, a telephone beside his bed that was directly linked with Washington rang sharply.

"Is that you, Ike?" a familiar voice asked. It was one of his many good friends in the Army, a colonel doing the same job for the current Chief of Staff that he himself had done for General MacArthur.

"Yes," Ike said, suddenly wide awake.

"The Chief says for you to hop a plane and get up here right away. Tell your boss that formal orders will come through later."

When Ike arrived, he was led to the office of General George C. Marshall, whom he'd met only briefly two or three times before. From the Virginia Military Institute, Marshall had risen to the highest post in the Army by showing a brilliant grasp of military strategy, but he was personally so reserved that some officers thought he lacked the human touch a successful commander needed. Yet he immediately impressed Eisenhower as a man who deserved his reputation for having outstanding mental abilities.

In scarcely fifteen minutes he gave Ike a brief but remarkably complete picture of the critical military situation confronting the United States as the result of Japan's surprise attack in the Pacific. Then he concluded with a question:

"What should be our general line of action?"

Eisenhower hesitated an instant before answering, "Give me a few hours."

Ike realized, of course, that he was being tested. He could not help feeling nervous when he returned to Marshall's office, so he spoke somewhat more carefully than usual as he summed up his ideas.

"General," he said, "it will be a long time before major reinforcements can go to the Philippines—longer than any garrison can hold out with driblet assistance, if the enemy commits major forces to their reduction. But we must do everything for them that is humanly possible. The people of China, the Philippines, the Dutch East Indies will be watching us. They may excuse failure, but they will not excuse abandonment. Their trust and friendship is important to us. Our base must be Australia and we must start at once to expand it and to secure our communications to it. In this last, we dare not fail. We must take great risks and spend any amount of money required."

Marshall nodded. "I agree with you," he said.

So Ike had passed this test, and it was General Marshall's turn to decide that here was a man who deserved the high praise other officers had given him.

For the next six months, they both had plenty of opportunity to confirm the opinions they'd formed during their first real encounter. In this period Ike worked almost around the clock outlining the specific steps to be taken toward getting America's war machine rolling. To start with, his duties as Assistant Chief of the War Plans Division of the Army involved concentrating on the fighting in the Pacific, where the United States was woefully weak owing to the losses it had suffered at the outbreak of hostilities.

Having spent five years in the Philippines, Ike felt a deep private hurt when the troops under General Mac-Arthur were forced to retreat there. But even before being promoted, in February of 1942, to the top post in the War Plans Division—directing the planning now for the American war effort in Europe as well as Asia—General Eisenhower fully subscribed to the basic principle of United States strategy.

Defeating the enemy in Europe must have top priority, he agreed. Only after Hitler surrendered could America concentrate on beating Japan.

Ike thought that any trained military officer must see the logic of this strategy. For Hitler had dared to take the bold step of attacking Soviet Russia, and the Red Army was desperately fighting hundreds of thousands of Nazi invaders. Even though France had been conquered in the frightful spring of 1940, when much of the rest of western Europe had also fallen into German hands, Britain under the bulldog leadership of Winston Churchill still defied Hitler. Thus, together with the British and

Canadians, the Free French, and the numerous smaller forces committed to destroying Nazism, the United States could teach Hitler a lesson every military academy stressed:

Don't fight on two different fronts at the same time if you can possibly help it.

The Allies could teach this lesson—and also win the war against Germany faster than by following any other strategy—if they started a second front in western Europe while the Russians were still keeping vast numbers of German soldiers very busy in the east.

The strategy was so obvious, in fact, that many people who knew nothing about warfare were urging it. "A SECOND FRONT NOW!" some newspapers demanded. Except for that small part of the public who refused to be distracted from considering Japan as the main enemy, most Americans began hoping early in 1942 that Allied forces would soon cross the English Channel and invade France.

Dwight Eisenhower held this hope, too—even though he knew better than all but a handful of top figures how unprepared the United States had been to fight even a limited war. During recent years a start had been made toward increasing the armed forces, and more than a million men had donned uniform before Pearl Harbor. Thousands more were being inducted every month, along with hundreds of women who would serve in many noncombat jobs. Meanwhile American industry was converting as speedily as possible to produce war supplies instead of cars and refrigerators. Nevertheless, Ike could see no chance of mustering sufficient troops, ships, and planes for any large-scale invasion at least until the spring of 1943.

But several of his superiors thought even that date was too optimistic. They supported the idea of striking a series of less powerful jabs at Nazi outposts, rather than trying for a knockout punch right away. Since President Roosevelt and Prime Minister Churchill also favored the more cautious policy for a variety of reasons, Ike was overruled.

Actually, he wasn't too disappointed personally. He had resigned himself to a desk job for the duration of the war, although he still yearned to command troops in combat. Did he mind the fact that hardly anybody outside the War Department knew how much he was contributing to the war effort? No, he didn't believe he craved any kind of fame among the general public. With two stars on his uniform now, he held the high rank of major general—and that was glory enough, he cheerfully assured his friends.

Still, he was delighted to be sent to London in the summer of 1942. At least he'd be closer to the action there, even if his duties weren't very different. Instead of doing his planning solely with American colleagues, he'd be dealing with the British, too, working out the details of the first Allied operation of this war—an invasion of North Africa. And, just by getting out of Washington, he thought he might stand a better chance of getting a field command sooner or later.

He got more than he bargained for.

When 150,000 American troops and 140,000 British troops landed in North Africa on November 8, 1942, their commanding officer was Lieutenant General Dwight Eisenhower.

Three months later, he was promoted to full general and received a fourth star . . .

The last Axis forces in Africa surrendered in May of 1943 . . .

In July, Ike commanded Allied troops in the invasion of Sicily . . .

The Italian mainland was invaded in September, and Italy surrendered . . .

Then finally, in the autumn of 1943, detailed planning began for the greatest military operation ever to be undertaken. At last the top leadership of the Allies felt strong enough to open a real second front. But the date for this massive invasion of Europe could not be announced, nor could the area to be attacked, nor any other fact that might possibly help Germany prepare its defenses.

Yet public clamor favoring such a decisive move had

grown so loud all over the free world that one important fact was disclosed in December. Whenever and wherever the Allies landed, there would be no secret about who was in charge. Obviously the Supreme Commander would be an American because the United States would provide by far the largest part of the manpower and equipment for the operation.

Many military men and some knowledgeable civilians expected that General Marshall would get the job as a well-deserved reward for his unsung service as Chief of Staff. Ike, too, felt sure that Marshall would be appointed, and that he himself would be assigned to the less glamorous duties of Chief of Staff. However, President Roosevelt, after all but settling on Marshall, called in the quiet Virginian, then threw up his hands. "I feel I could not sleep at night with you out of the country," FDR said.

Then, a few days later, riding in a jeep beside General Eisenhower to inspect some troops, Roosevelt told him with a jaunty smile: "Well, Ike, you are going to command OVERLORD."

8 OVERLORD

Eisenhower had already been carrying a heavy burden of responsibility for two years. Although he looked much younger, he was in his early fifties now, and sometimes his face betrayed how tired he felt. But as soon as he heard about his awesome new assignment, he plunged into a series of tense conferences with the same zest he'd once shown on the football field.

So he couldn't help grinning when he received a scolding cable from General Marshall:

You will be under terrific strain from now on. I am interested that you are fully prepared to bear the strain and I am not interested in the usual rejoinder that you can take it. It is of vast importance that you be fresh mentally and you certainly will not be if you go straight from one great problem to another. Now come on home and see your wife and trust somebody else for twenty minutes in England.

General Eisenhower and President Roosevelt on a trip to the battlefront.

Of course, Ike obeyed the order. However, the newspapers back in the United States had been printing his picture so often lately that people might recognize him if they caught a glimpse of him—and the fact that he was taking a vacation would surely interest the German High Command. Therefore the Chief of Staff arranged for him to travel behind drawn shades to visit his mother in Kansas and his son, who was following in his own footsteps by attending West Point. Marshall also saw to it that Mamie Eisenhower was whisked to a secluded cottage at White Sulphur Springs in West Virginia, where she and her husband had a happy, uninterrupted reunion.

All this thoughtfulness, from a man who was supposed to be lacking in human feeling, touched Ike deeply, especially because he realized that Marshall must be disappointed about having to stay in Washington. Modest as he was, he still must have wanted his own chance to go down in history by leading the invasion of Europe.

For OVERLORD, as its code name suggested, would be the biggest military operation ever to be attempted. More than *2 million* men would storm the beaches of France, and to transport them across the English Channel would require the largest armada of ships ever assembled. As a shield for this vast convoy thousands of planes would sweep the skies, while others attacked German strongpoints near the coastline.

Was Dwight Eisenhower really capable of directing such an immense undertaking?

That he had one of the basic qualities any successful general must possess was obvious at first glance. While he wasn't imposing in his appearance the way General MacArthur was, Ike practically radiated warmth and enthusiasm when he met people in person. Even his photographs transmitted a good part of this appeal. Somehow he made perfect strangers more than willing to accept his leadership.

Stiff-mannered Britishers liked him as much as easy-going Americans did. What's more, they trusted him because he seemed unable to pretend or to tell even polite lies, and gave the impression of measuring his every judgment by the simple test of when a particular action would help or hurt the Allied cause. Actually, some people scoffed that Ike was too simple in his outlook. It wasn't as easy as he apparently thought it was to distinguish between right and wrong, they said. But in the wartime climate, where defeating the enemy took precedence over any private concern, most people found Ike's simplicity refreshing.

And not only was his personality remarkably attractive. He had already proved amply in North Africa and Italy that he could make hard military decisions when he had to. He also kept demonstrating, month after month, that he had a sure instinct for keeping his troops from feeling that nobody cared about their welfare. For instance, he heard during an inspection trip that a lot of foot soldiers were muttering complaints because a brigadier general had set up a plush rest camp on the isle of Capri open just to American Air Force officers. Ike's temper exploded then with an immediate order opening the resort to "*all* British and American personnel in this area, particularly from combat units."

So the men and women Ike commanded never gave him a sarcastic nickname of the sort that many other officers got. Even when General Eisenhower visited troops who soon would have to wade ashore facing a frightful rain of German artillery fire, they always greeted him with cheers, then surrounded him seeking his autograph.

If Ike ever worried about whether the invasion of France might fail, he did not say so. Yet he wrote in a sort of diary that he felt strangely alone, despite having dozens of aides working with him at his headquarters. For nobody else could really share his blame if something important went wrong. Although he had personally selected most of the high officers who would lead the assault on D-Day, only he himself could give the crucial signal: "Let's go!" What if the weather turned stormy after the great armada was launched? As the target date came closer, however, Ike told himself that any commander had to believe, above all, in his own luck. "Of course," he mused to one of his top aides, "anybody can draw a bad card sometimes."

But Ike's marvelous luck held on June 6, 1944.

On that morning, the radios in millions of American homes crackled with thrilling news. D-Day had arrived at last. A vast Allied force was landing at several points along the French coast. Despite heavy German fire, the Allies were advancing. That evening President Roosevelt led the nation in a prayer for the safety of the loved ones who were fighting on the beaches of France. As in all wars, there would be many families whose prayers were in vain—but Allied casualties were less severe than had been feared.

And week after week, for the next eleven months, General Eisenhower's troops pushed the Germans relentlessly back toward their own country. At times the advance slowed or even was halted, causing doleful headlines.

Still, the Allies recovered every loss . . .

They set Paris free . . .

They reached the Rhine River . . .

Then, as the Russians pressed westward beyond the Soviet borders and the Allies raced eastward into Germany, Adolf Hitler took his own life . . .

The German generals surrendered . . .

And on May 8, 1945, the war in Europe ended!

No man was more relieved to have the fighting over

than Dwight Eisenhower. Almost instantly it became clear, though, that millions of other people whose spirits had also soared with the news of the Allied victory shared a feeling among themselves that he found amazing. They seemed determined to treat him as if he'd beaten Hitler all by himself.

At the invitation of Winston Churchill, Ike flew to London for a ceremony presenting him with a key to the city. Weren't the British supposed to behave rather stand-offishly? Not on this occasion. Tens of thousands of them swarmed from the sidewalks into the roadways, striving to shake his hand as he was driven through the streets of the old city.

"I am not a native of this land," Eisenhower said in his speech of acceptance. "I come from the very heart of America. . . ." Then his simple words about the importance of continued cooperation between Britain and the United States to defeat Japan and to preserve world peace were repeatedly cheered by his staid audience.

But not until Ike landed in Washington, for what he expected to be a brief and restful visit, did he begin to grasp what lay in store for him. As he stepped off his plane, reporters rushed to overhear his first words to Mamie and General Marshall. Despite being nearly surrounded, the three of them managed to climb into a waiting jeep, Ike sitting up front beside the driver. An enormous crowd had gathered behind the airport gates, and from the jeep's back seat General Marshall quietly suggested, "Stand up so they can see you."

Ike not only stood, he also did what came naturally: he grinned and waved to the throngs lining his route—in Washington . . . New York . . . Kansas City . . .

Everywhere, the outpouring of emotion astonished him, although hardboiled newsmen told him he shouldn't be surprised. "You're just getting a hero's welcome," they explained, but still Ike shook his head. If he could have heard what they said in private, he'd have shaken his head even harder. "This man is absolutely a natural for the White House," they were telling each other.

Soon enough, the subject was raised to Ike himself—by none other than President Harry Truman. In office barely a month, following the death of Franklin Roosevelt during the final weeks of the fighting with Germany, the former Vice President flew to Europe shortly after Ike returned to duty there. Truman came to attend a summit meeting of Allied leaders, and possibly he felt some of the same qualms about his own abilities that many other people felt.

For FDR had been President longer than anybody else in American history, having won a fourth term on the last previous Election Day. And he'd been a strong President, who had dominated American politics since 1932. Although General Eisenhower had privately disliked many of Roosevelt's policies, he'd considered FDR a

General Eisenhower waving to crowds in New York City's parade welcoming him home after the war in Europe ended.

great war leader, along with the majority of his fellow citizens. So he couldn't help sharing the widespread dismay when someone the newspapers called "the little man from Missouri" suddenly became the most powerful man in the whole free world.

But whether or not Truman did feel up to the job, he certainly astounded Ike one afternoon while they were riding in a car together on their way to attend a session of the Potsdam Conference near Berlin.

"General," Truman said, "there is nothing that you may want that I won't try to help you get. *That definitely and specifically includes the Presidency in 1948.*"

Ike burst out laughing, he later told some friends. Even though his post as Supreme Commander had inevitably involved making many decisions with political overtones, he had always thought of himself as a person with no real interest in politics. He never gave any interviewer the slightest clue about which political party he supported. Nevertheless, in his own mind he was a convinced Republican, and of course he was well aware that Truman was a Democrat.

"Mr. President," Eisenhower said when he stopped laughing, "I don't know who will be your opponent for the Presidency in 1948, but it won't be me."

So now Harry Truman knew something most Americans could not know—that Ike was definitely not a Democrat. And Ike had also learned something rather surprising—that Truman was willing to step aside instead of running for a full term in the next election campaign, as most people expected. What could be the reason? Ike didn't need any great political skill to answer his own question. Truman obviously must believe that no other candidate stood a better chance of winning for the Democrats in 1948 than Dwight Eisenhower.

Put it another way, a few close friends of Ike's suggested. Maybe Truman wanted to make sure that General Eisenhower wasn't going to run as a Republican—in which case no Democrat on earth could win.

However, this kind of talk irritated Ike, and he asked his friends to stop it. Naturally any good citizen would be proud to serve as President, and if his fellow Americans were to choose him for this great honor he would surely do his best. But the pushing and shoving of party politics was a dirty game he wasn't getting into if he could possibly avoid it. Besides, hadn't he already done his share of public service?

Indeed he had, Ike and Mamie both agreed. He'd spent the past thirty years wearing the uniform of an Army officer, the past four of them under extraordinary pressures. At the age of fifty-four, he felt entitled to spend whatever time remained to him enjoying some of the pleasures of private life that he'd never yet tasted.

Since President Truman had asked him to set up a system for governing the conquered Germany, Ike would do this while other generals finished the war against Japan. But as soon as possible after peace came, he'd retire from active duty. Why, in all of those years he and Mamie had kept moving all over the map, without ever having a real home of their own. Now they'd buy some land, and a nice roomy old house because their son was talking about getting married, so one of these days they might be grandparents needing plenty of space for little visitors.

Ike still had too much energy, though, to be able to look forward to just relaxing, and even he couldn't play golf more than a couple of times a week. A fine idea for keeping his mind alert, while possibly being of some use, had occurred to him. He couldn't imagine taking on any such fancy title as professor, yet it seemed to him that he might have a few words of wisdom to offer today's young people.

Then wouldn't it make sense to plan on settling near some little college town?

When Japan surrendered in August of 1945, that's what Ike and Mamie were ready to do.

9 WHAT LITTLE COLLEGE TOWN?

But General Eisenhower could not simply retire from the great stage on which he'd played such a major role during the past four years. For there were many decisions affecting the whole world's future that remained to be made, and he was one of the few men qualified to help in making them.

Not that Ike's opinions were always heeded by the Allies' top leaders. On the most fateful question of recent years—and possibly of all time—his advice had been ignored. He'd known, of course, about the secret project to develop an atomic weapon, and at the Potsdam Conference he'd learned along with other high-ranking officials that the first test bomb had just been exploded in the New Mexico desert. But he was appalled to hear that President Truman planned to use the awful new bomb against Japan.

Why must the United States do something so "horrible

and destructive?" Ike asked Secretary of War Stimson. Public opinion everywhere would be shocked, he insisted. And even though Eisenhower wasn't intimately familiar with the situation in the Far East, it seemed to him that surely Japan was almost beaten already.

Nevertheless, other advisors told Truman an atomic attack would save lives in the long run by shortening the war, and the President agreed with them. Whether the terrible explosions over Hiroshima and Nagasaki should have been ordered would be debated endlessly thereafter, but the unleashing of atomic power did make Japan surrender within a few days. While Ike rejoiced at the coming of peace, his misgivings about the way it had been gained could not be forgotten.

In his own European sphere, a new atmosphere of suspicion made his dealings with the Russians much more difficult. Would the wartime friendship between the United States and the Soviet Union have chilled inevitably even if no atomic rivalry had developed? This was another question that would stir many debates during the next several decades.

Privately, Ike gave a friend his own feeling in 1945. "Before the atom bomb was used," he confided, "I would have said, yes, I was sure we could keep the peace with Russia. I would have said that we three, Britain with her mighty fleet, America with the strongest air force, and Russia with the strongest land force, we three could have guaranteed the peace of the world for a long, long time to come. But now, I don't know. Everyone feels insecure again."

So within just a few months after the end of the shooting, a new sort of struggle had started. The "Cold War" it was called, and in this contest the United States and the Soviet Union were the main antagonists.

Yet Ike's personal experiences with the Russians had been so warm and friendly that he thought the drift toward conflict might still be stopped. By now he'd returned to Washington for a final tour of duty as Chief of Staff before he took off his uniform for good. Because he felt obliged to do what he could to prod Congress into passing two important measures, he'd heeded President Truman's request that he end his career this way, while General Marshall went on a special mission to China. One of the bills Ike wanted to see adopted would unify the Army and Navy for greater efficiency under the control of a single Department of Defense. The other would set up a peacetime draft to make sure the armed forces did not shrink as they had after World War I, endangering the nation's security.

But he also proposed an idea for decreasing tension with the Soviet Union. We ought to share our atomic knowledge with the Russians, General Eisenhower suggested.

One senator after another angrily objected, while some

who didn't anger as easily spoke in pitying tones. "Ike is like a babe in arms when it comes to politics," they said. The few who weren't either furious or sarcastic were easily drowned out by their louder colleagues.

So hardly anybody heard Ike explain that scientists said it was only a matter of time till the Russians developed atomic bombs of their own. "Let's be realistic," Ike said. "Other nations will get the secret anyway. There is some point in making a virtue of necessity." In short, why not try trusting the Russians? At best, this might convince them that the United States in turn could be trusted and was not bent on wiping out Communism. At worst, they'd have the weapon just a little sooner than they'd get it on their own. To mutter about its being unpatriotic to help a potential enemy was plain nonsense, in Ike's mind.

Yet he had less taste than ever for arguing political questions in public. The furor he stirred on Capitol Hill by just a few remarks made him increasingly anxious to leave this quarrelsome scene. As the months passed he felt still more fed up, and he and Mamie talked more seriously about looking for a farm. But they still hadn't gotten around to doing it when Ike was approached with a startling request.

As soon as he retired, would he take the post of president of Columbia University in New York City?

"You must have the wrong Eisenhower," Ike told his

caller with a broad grin. "It must be Milton you want." For his youngest brother was the college president in the family, having made a distinguished record as head of Kansas State before moving on to the greater challenge of Penn State. Actually, the general noted, Milton would be a fine choice for Columbia's trustees if they wanted an outstanding figure to head their world-famed institution.

No, it was Ike they wanted, the chairman of the trustees insisted.

Well, he'd certainly had some remarkable offers since he'd returned from Europe, Ike said, but this took the cake. Why, he knew nothing about higher education, not having had any himself except what he'd got at West Point. And in his day there, most of the courses had been on military subjects. How could he hold his head up in a room full of professors, let alone address them as their boss?

Nevertheless, the trustees persisted. There were plenty of deans to supervise academic matters, they said. But for the presidency of the university they wanted an able administrator, and Ike surely filled that bill. They also needed a man who could speak at select gatherings around the country, telling well-off individuals why Columbia needed a lot of money—telling the story in a way that would make them listen, then write sizable checks. Because of his great personal popularity Ike was bound to be a better money-raiser than anyone else they could think of, the trustees kept saying.

So Ike let himself be convinced. After all, to help a great learning center get back on its feet financially was a worthy cause, he explained to Mamie. While he'd had dozens of other job offers, he didn't think it was right to lend his name to any business venture. Except for writing a book about his war experiences, which would probably be of real use to historians, he wouldn't use his prestige as a war leader to put money in his own pocket.

Having made up his mind, Ike resigned from active duty in the Army in February of 1948. It was an emotional moment when he took off his uniform with its five silver stars on the shoulder—a special five-star rank had been created by Congress to honor a handful of top officers. He immediately plunged into the new and absorbing project of compiling his personal history of the war. Dictating to three secretaries working in a sort of relay system, while a team of researchers checked facts for him, he finished his *Crusade in Europe* in record time. Soon he was reaping a profit of around a half million dollars as the book soared to the top of the best-seller list.

By then, Ike and Mamie were uncomfortably settled in a gloomy old mansion in New York City. This house, reserved for the use of Columbia's president, depressed them with its dark wood paneling and ornate marble mantels. The only room where Ike felt at ease was an airy little "penthouse" on the roof, which they fixed up as his hideaway.

When Mamie was having her portrait painted, the artist set up his easel there to take advantage of the natural light. Just for fun, Ike picked up a paintbrush one afternoon while Mamie and the artist were searching the rest of the house to find a place where the finished portrait could be hung. They discovered him dabbling contentedly on a piece of cardboard box, and the next day a parcel was delivered to Ike. It contained a complete supply of painting materials, with the artist's compliments.

So Ike spent some happy hours up on the roof enjoying his new hobby. He also had a good time helping Coach Lou Little with the Columbia football team.

Yet he felt like a fish out of water during most of his campus stay, and he soon realized he'd made a mistake.

Even if certain professors thought he was pretty dumb, he was smart enough to see that so-called intellectuals usually looked down on soldiers as inferior creatures. For that matter, he really couldn't feel at ease with most professors—their worlds were too different—and the quicker he moved on, the better off they'd all be.

Thus Ike was more than ready to answer a new call from President Truman in the autumn of 1950. Despite

Columbia's football team getting some pointers from a former player.

the widespread belief that Truman couldn't possibly get elected, he'd surprised everybody by beating New York's Governor Dewey two years earlier. Among the policies Truman was pressing, one made a lot of sense to Ike, and he'd testified in Washington in favor of a treaty setting up a peacetime alliance with several European countries. Now NATO—as the North Atlantic Treaty Organization was called—was ready to establish a joint military defense force over in Europe, and Truman wanted General Eisenhower as its commander.

Ike took the job not merely as a graceful way of leaving Columbia. He also had his private reasons for wanting to wear his uniform again. Even though he'd thought it would be a great relief to move out of the inner circle where momentous decisions were made, he found himself missing the excitement he'd thrived on for six years. Civilian life didn't really suit him, he guessed. Furthermore, his uniform was a fine protection against the temptation to get involved in politics.

For a lot of people were still talking to him about the White House, and it was starting to sound more appealing. Many of the rich men he'd met while raising money for Columbia were Republicans who kept urging him to run. They joked about his refusal in 1948 as being a prime example of "the Eisenhower luck"—because in that year the spunky Truman might have beaten even him.

But in 1952 Ike just could not lose, they said, and Ike found himself listening with increasing interest.

Yet he didn't really want to be President, he was still telling friends. And if he went back on active duty all this political talk would have to quiet down. For it was a rule in the official Army regulations that no officer could actively seek any elective office. So that was that, Ike seemed to be saying as he put on his uniform again in December of 1950.

10 CANDIDATE IKE

But letters about political topics kept arriving at General Eisenhower's new headquarters near Paris. Friends came to visit him there, bringing urgent messages from Republican Party leaders. Throughout 1951, Ike repeatedly told these friends to spread the word that he was not seeking the Presidency.

No, he would not *seek* this high office, he insisted—and yet a lot of people he didn't even know seemed set on seeking it for him. Some Republicans on the Pacific Coast formed a group called Citizens for Eisenhower, while "I Like Ike" clubs sprang up all over the country. Whether or not he wanted to run, it appeared that he was widely being considered as a candidate in 1952.

Of course, he could have followed the example set by the famous Civil War general William Tecumseh Sherman. When political leaders of his day had pressed Sherman to try for the White House, he'd said flatly, "If nominated I will not run; if elected I will not serve." Ever since then, anybody who really meant to shut the door on a political career had only to repeat Sherman's blunt statement.

However, Eisenhower issued no such statement. What he did was to give his visitors a variety of rather confusing comments about "higher duty" and his reluctance either to strive for it or to avoid it. In his own mind, though, he thought his meaning was plain. If a majority of his countrymen truly wished to have him as their President, he'd accept their verdict—but he would not lift a finger to fight for the job.

Then you won't get it!

That's what Ike's closest political friends finally got up the nerve to tell him in the opening months of 1952. Daring his well-known hot temper, they informed him that not even a great war hero could simply be lifted into the White House without any effort on his part. They reminded him that other men who had devoted their whole lives to politics would fight hard to get nominated. Senator Robert Taft, the unofficial head of the Republican Party, would certainly not step aside at the coming convention because some delegates were wearing "I Like Ike" buttons. Taft had been working for nearly four years to sew up convention votes, and his supporters were claiming that Ike wasn't even a Republican.

So unless Ike came home and started making some

political speeches right away, he wouldn't stand a chance of getting nominated, let alone elected.

Ike's neck turned red while he listened, a sure sign that his temper was ready to explode. But within a few weeks he had resigned from the Army and returned to the United States. In July of 1952, the Republican National Convention nominated him as its candidate for President.

Then Dwight Eisenhower proved once again that when he entered any contest, he was determined to win it. Hardly anybody expected him to have the slightest trouble getting elected because the Democrats had chosen the little-known Governor of Illinois to oppose him. But Adlai Stevenson, promising to "talk sense to the American people," suddenly began stirring some excitement.

Besides speaking thoughtfully about such problems as civil rights, Stevenson also displayed a quick wit that endeared him to most of the reporters covering the campaign. Both his ideas and his sense of humor strongly attracted a portion of the public that prided itself on its intelligence. For instance Stevenson, being noticeably bald, quipped that he was proud to be the candidate of the "eggheads."

Ike, despite his own thinning hair, definitely belonged in a different category. As the campaign progressed, he kept sinking lower in the estimate of eggheads. By picking Richard Nixon as his running mate, he upset many liberals who thought the thirty-nine-year-old Senator from California had used dirty tricks to win his Senate seat. Then, when the *New York Post* disclosed that Nixon had accepted illegal money gifts, Ike upset these liberals even more by letting his candidate for Vice President "explain" on television that he hadn't knowingly accepted any gift except his dog, Checkers.

But Ike's failure to defend another man disturbed even some conservatives.

The man was General George Marshall, who'd done so much to further Eisenhower's own career. During Marshall's postwar service as Secretary of State, he'd earned the hatred of one of the most amazing figures in American political history—Senator Joseph McCarthy of Wisconsin. In whipping up a frenzy of anti-Red feeling, McCarthy wildly charged in the autumn of 1952 that General Marshall was an outright traitor who had put Russia's interests ahead of those of the United States. Of course, Eisenhower knew this was nonsense—very dangerous nonsense—and, after much badgering by reporters, he decided to speak up in Marshall's defense. He wrote a paragraph upholding Marshall's patriotism into a speech planned for delivery in Milwaukee. Advance copies of the speech had already been handed to newsmen when

Eisenhower met with a group of high-level Republicans. At their urging, he did not read his paragraph about General Marshall when he gave his speech.

This action, or lack of action, depressed many Democrats. For despite Stevenson's best efforts, it seemed increasingly clear as the election approached that he would not win. Every poll showed that most people didn't like the "egghead" label—and that, regardless of their usual political persuasion, they did like Ike. Then why did Eisenhower feel obliged to pay so much attention to the opinions of extreme right-wing Republicans?

Because he'd been bit by the Presidential bug after all, some reporters said—so he'd do whatever he thought he had to, just to make sure he didn't lose. And it couldn't really be denied that McCarthy and Nixon, with their drive to "purge" the country of any Communist taint, had aroused a lot of voters.

But McCarthy was trying to tear up the Constitution, other writers insisted. Even if Ike was no deep thinker on political issues, he ought to be aware that freedom of speech would disappear unless McCarthy's reckless attacks on anybody who disagreed with him could be stopped. It was impossible to imagine that Ike would purposely mislead the public. So his strange silence in Milwaukee must mean that he really held extremely right-wing opinions himself.

Every attempt to make Eisenhower disclose exactly

Ike's wife—one of his strongest supporters when he ran for President.

where he stood on any specific issue was met with the same kind of good-natured but fuzzy response. His campaign speeches were mostly hazy promises about "cleaning up the mess" in Washington that the Democrats had created during the past twenty years. Yet, on November 4, he was elected President by a margin of more than 5 million votes.

11 MR. PRESIDENT

On January 20, 1953, Dwight David Eisenhower took office as President of the United States. Even before being sworn in, he had already carried out one of the few specific promises he'd made during the campaign. "I shall go to Korea," he'd said, and these five words had been credited with swaying millions of voters.

For the nation was involved in another war now—a war that nobody wanted and that it seemed increasingly sure nobody could win. Since the summer of 1950, American soldiers had been dying in distant Korea, supposedly to teach a basic lesson to the leaders of the Soviet Union.

To President Truman and his advisors, it had been absolutely clear that the Communist rulers of Russia had pulled the strings when three years ago an army of North Koreans had invaded South Korea. In the politically tense aftermath of World War II, the northern part of this Asian country had come under the unofficial protection of Moscow, while the southern part relied in the same way on Washington.

Truman had felt that he must not permit any Soviet puppets to take over the whole of Korea. Up till then his Cold War strategy for keeping the Russians from expanding their influence had appeared to be succeeding without the loss of any lives. A lot of money had been spent on helping friendly nations, on building air bases, on testing weapons, but the policy would be a failure if we refused to fight when one of our friends was attacked, Truman had told the American people.

And the great majority—Republicans as well as Democrats—had agreed with him at first. Although Truman had gone through the motions of getting the new United Nations to sponsor a "police action" in Korea, there could be no doubt that this was really an American operation. As such, it inevitably became a major issue in American politics.

By the time Eisenhower started to make political speeches, Korea had turned into "a terrible can of worms," as experienced political figures put it. The Republicans had been claiming that they were more anti-Communist then any Democrat could be, and yet they blamed Truman for getting involved in Korea. He should have made the South Koreans so strong that the North Koreans wouldn't have dared to start trouble, Republicans in Congress had been saying. They also said that once the United States had entered the fighting, it should have fought to win, using atom bombs if necessary, instead of letting the conflict drag on so long. Not having their own man in the White House, they didn't have to worry about whether or not such action might provoke an awful nuclear war.

But Eisenhower would have to worry about this if he won. So what would he do to end the Korean stalemate?

"I shall go to Korea," he said—and the mere promise satisfied millions of people. Then pictures of Ike, back in uniform temporarily, inspecting the battlefront soon after he was elected, provided further reassurance. Hadn't General Eisenhower beaten Hitler? Now surely he'd find a way to stop this senseless fighting over in Asia, which had already killed more than 30,000 American boys.

Yet it took President Eisenhower six months to announce an armistice in Korea, and the terms he accepted raised the eyebrows of thoughtful people in both political parties. In effect, he agreed to the same situation that had prevailed before the fighting started, with no advantage gained for the cause of freedom despite the loss of so many lives and the spending of billions of dollars on weapons. "If Truman had signed anything like this, the Republicans would have impeached him," Capitol Hill correspondents told each other.

However, the main reaction throughout the country was a great sense of relief. Most men and women seemed to feel that with Ike in the White House they could stop worrying about the problems of the world. After so many years of crisis—ever since the 1930s—they welcomed a chance to concentrate on their own personal concerns.

They were delighted to see pictures of Ike playing with his grandchildren or playing golf. When Mamie got busy directing the remodeling of an old farmhouse near Gettysburg in Pennsylvania, everybody approved. Wasn't it nice that, after all the years of moving around, Ike and his wife were finally going to have a home of their own to enjoy after they left Washington?

Not very many people bothered to read much about dreary matters such as the federal budget. Ike had brought numerous businessmen into his government, and they eased many of the rules and regulations that had hampered business under the Democrats. "What's good for General Motors is good for the country," Ike's new Secretary of Defense, who'd been president of General Motors, had told Senators looking into whether he'd feel any conflict of interest when he took over as boss at the Pentagon. People had laughed at the remark, but there appeared to be some sense in it because the country was certainly prospering.

So only a handful of diehard Republicans complained that instead of balancing the budget, as he'd promised, President Eisenhower was adding to the deficit. They had to admit, though, that they wouldn't support any cut in military spending, with the Russians still such a menace. Nor did they really believe it would be politically feasible to cut out all the New Deal programs—such as unemployment insurance—much as they'd like to.

At the same time, only diehard Democrats complained about Ike's disinterest in domestic problems, particularly the rising pressure brought by young black Americans demanding equal rights. When the Supreme Court issued its history-making decision outlawing segregated schools, liberals muttered that a President should do more to give the nation moral leadership as it entered a new era than just saying it was his duty to see that all laws were enforced.

Yet how much enforcing did he do? People with a special interest in the operation of the government noted that President Eisenhower seemed to be less involved personally with the immense responsibilities of his office than any other White House occupant in memory. Following the system he'd learned in the Army, he had appointed Governor Sherman Adams of New Hampshire as his "chief of staff." With the new title of Assistant to the President, Adams headed an Army-style chain of command along which instructions were relayed and reports made. Only brief summaries of the most important matters went to the President for him to act on himself.

While Harry Truman had still been in the White House, he'd predicted what would happen when his successor took over. "He'll sit here," Truman had said, tapping his chair, "and he'll say, 'Do this!' 'Do that!' *And nothing will happen*. Poor Ike—it won't be a bit like the Army. He'll find it very frustrating."

Eisenhower had his own idea, though, about the value of his system. "Now, look," he told one of his speech-writers who wanted him to take a stronger position on some issue. "I happen to *know* a little about leadership. I've had to work with a lot of nations, for that matter, at odds with each other. And I tell you this: you do not *lead* by hitting people over the head. Leadership is *persuasion* —and *education*—and *patience*. It's long, slow, tough work."

And from his own vantage point, his first years in the White House were anything but dull. Despite the general feeling in the country that nothing much was happening, Eisenhower devoted more energy than most people imagined to dealing with foreign problems. From Iran to Guatemala, he kept challenging the Russians all around the world.

As his Secretary of State, he'd appointed a sour-looking lawyer named John Foster Dulles. Most people thought it was Dulles who was really fighting the Cold War even more forcefully than Truman had dared, while Ike made soothing statements about keeping the peace when tension mounted too much. But why would Eisenhower allow one of his aides to follow a policy he himself did not believe in?

He was lazy, many Democrats said. He needed the support of the Republican right wing, others decided. Only after the private documents of his administration became available to the writers of history would a new idea about Ike be proposed.

At least in foreign affairs, these papers suggested, President Eisenhower took a far more active part than most observers surmised while he was in the White House. Apparently, every sharp statement that Dulles made had been discussed in advance, for Ike had developed some strong opinions about the best method for getting along with the Russians. His mind had changed greatly since the days when he'd thought they could be trusted. Now his main object was to limit their influence in every possible way, at the same time expanding the influence of the United States.

So he was very tired as he departed for Denver late in the summer of 1955 to spend a few weeks resting at the home of his wife's family. Despite all the afternoons he'd spent on the golf course, he'd been under great strain for several years. Although he still looked more vigorous than many younger men, he was almost sixty-four.

Yet the country was stunned to hear the news, in the middle of September, that President Eisenhower had just suffered a heart attack.

12 "MUCH BETTER, THANKS."

The first bulletins caused great anxiety. With the President in an oxygen tent, how would the country be governed? Should Vice President Nixon take over unofficially, and if so, who was to decide how long such an arrangement should last?

For within just a few hours, the President's doctors gave the hopeful opinion that he seemed on the road to recovery. However, it might take several months until he could get back to his desk. In a hasty series of meetings, the men who were closest to Eisenhower made a rather surprising decision: not to give Richard Nixon any extra duties, no matter that he still might inherit one of the world's hardest jobs at any moment.

So the Vice President, apparently, wasn't very popular among the White House advisors. Ever since he had squirmed out of the scandal about accepting doubtful gifts of money during the 1952 campaign, using his little dog to win public sympathy, a lot of people had been calling him "Tricky Dick." Yet the death of Senator Taft, and the sudden downfall of Senator McCarthy after the whole Senate had voted to censure him, had left Nixon as the leading figure in the right wing of the Republican Party. Nevertheless, he was practically ignored by the inner circle that conducted the country's essential business while President Eisenhower remained a hospital patient.

To reassure the public, Eisenhower's press secretary gave out lengthy reports three times every day, describing the President's condition in complete detail. Even more reassuringly, a photo was soon passed around showing a smiling Ike, sitting chipperly in a wheelchair, wearing a shirt with a cheerful message embroidered across the chest: "Much better, thanks."

Indeed, he felt so well that he returned to Washington less than six weeks after being stricken. Although he did not resume his full schedule for another several weeks, one of the capital's favorite games began again unbelievably soon.

Would Ike run for a second term?

To guess the answer to this question occupied the best minds in the world of politics until Ike himself broke the suspense at the end of February in the election year of 1956. Then he finally told a press conference that he'd decided, yes, he'd heed the call of duty once again.

That didn't stop the guessing game, though. Instead the question shifted to: Who will be the next Vice President? For rumor had it that Ike had made up his mind to "dump" Nixon, despite the anger this would stir among the most conservative members of his party.

The rumor proved to have some basis, as Nixon himself admitted in a book he wrote a few years later. Nixon said that Ike had called him in and asked if the younger man wouldn't prefer some other post during the next four years. Considering that the President who was asking the question was sixty-five and not in the best of health, Nixon quite understandably could not think of a job he'd rather have than that of Vice President.

Eisenhower still could have picked someone else, but he did not. He also did not change his mind about running again himself—not even after another health emergency. Less than three months before the Republican Convention he suffered severe pains, and his doctors told him that he had an intestinal ailment called ileitis. They operated on him in the middle of a night early in June—then, at the end of August, his party formally named him to run for another term.

And on November 6, 1956, the American people once more chose Dwight Eisenhower as their President instead of Adlai Stevenson—this time by a margin of nearly 10 million votes.

13 TURNING POINTS

Right from the start of President Eisenhower's second term, events seemed to conspire against him. Business conditions worsened, riots erupted, the Russians scored a notable triumph by launching the first manmade satellite ever to orbit around the earth.

And for the first time in his career, Ike suffered an experience few people in public life escape. Although he thought he'd grown accustomed to being criticized since he'd entered politics, actually he'd been treated very kindly until now by the press and by his political opponents. His popularity among the people of the country had prevented any sharp attacks. But during 1957, his popularity sagged noticeably.

In January of that year, as he was beginning his second term, a Gallup poll showed that 79 per cent of the American people approved of the way he was doing his job. By November, the number who approved had shrunk to 57 per cent. Though this was still a majority, the Eisenhower magic did seem to be losing its power.

Even his closest aides found it hard to defend Ike's handling of the domestic troubles that arose during the year—especially the severe racial crisis in Little Rock, Arkansas. Opposition to the Supreme Court decision ordering an end to segregated schools had been simmering for many months in the South, and it came to a boil after a judge ordered that Little Rock's Central High School must admit nine black children. With the support of Arkansas state officials, angry whites shouting curses promised they would fight any effort to comply with the judge's ruling.

At a press conference, President Eisenhower was asked whether he would use federal troops to enforce the integration of public schools in the South. After several indecisive sentences about how much reliance he put on the "common sense" of the American people he finally came out with a remark that encouraged the racists. "I can't imagine any set of circumstances that would ever induce me to send federal troops," he said.

Yet ten days later, after screaming whites had rioted for three hours in Little Rock's streets, the President found it necessary to send paratroopers to that city so that nine black children could safely enter the school building.

Thus Eisenhower seemed to be proving that he could

President Eisenhower with Martin Luther King, Jr., and other
civil rights leaders at the White House.

not be counted on to provide any forceful leadership during a crucial turning point in the nation's troubled racial history. Only after young blacks opened a campaign of nonviolent "sit-in's," aimed at integrating lunch counters, did he finally heed advice from the one black on his White House staff. Then he invited Martin Luther King, Jr., and a delegation of other important figures in the nonviolence movement to meet with him. Since this was the first time any group of black leaders had ever been welcomed to the White House, liberals hoped it might signal a new attitude on the President's part. But nothing more happened and their hopes gradually faded.

At the same time, labor union members became increasingly disenchanted. But how could a President who had so many friends in the ranks of big business be expected to sympathize very deeply with the plight of the unemployed? And with more men and women losing their jobs every month, a recession—if not a depression—was surely on the way.

Even the most stalwart admirers of President Eisenhower had their confidence shaken by a puzzling scandal during his second term. Ike's closest aide, the stern Sherman Adams who had often lectured the Democrats on "the mess" they had created in Washington while they had run the government, suddenly turned up in the headlines. For Adams admitted accepting some suspicious gifts. At first Ike defended him—then, as if he really could not make up his mind about anything, he asked Adams to resign.

Yet it was in the field of foreign affairs, where Eisenhower was supposedly strongest, that he suffered his most serious loss of prestige. When the Russians launched their first Sputnik, as they called their space satellite, it stirred a great debate.

What was wrong with the way science was taught in American schools? For there must be something wrong, most people seemed to believe, if the Soviets could accomplish something so exciting while the United States didn't even have a space program.

Nevertheless, the underlying reason why Sputnik made such a deep impression proved to be more than a spirit of competition. In numerous ways during the late 1950s, the American people showed a growing doubt about the basic premise of Eisenhower's foreign policy— they seemed to be getting tired, at last, of the Cold War.

Instead of challenging the Russians or the Red Chinese every few months about who should have more influence over some distant spot of land, it appeared, a lot of people preferred doing the challenging peacefully, in outer space. Reacting to this feeling, Eisenhower appointed a special assistant to advise the White House on science and space technology.

More important, since he'd always considered himself a man committed to peace rather than war, he decided that there might be some point after all in meeting personally with Russia's Premier, Nikita Khrushchev. So he invited the Communist leader to visit the United States. Although Ike seemed not too happy as he greeted Khrushchev, he and the bouncy Russian got along much better than he'd expected. Khrushchev ended his farewell speech to the American people, carried all over the country on television, by waving his Russian interpreter aside. "Goodbye, good luck, friends!" the Soviet Premier cried in English.

So a surge of hope about the prospects for world peace arose everywhere during the closing months of 1959. However, it was dashed when spring came and an astounding news bulletin flashed around the world. The Soviet Union announced it had shot down an American spy plane as it flew over Russian territory snapping pictures with a special camera capable of taking detailed photographs from a very high altitude.

Could this be true?

President Eisenhower denied it—and then the Russians produced some pictures of their own, showing the wrecked plane with its special equipment. They also produced the American pilot, who had miraculously survived the plane's crash.

So Ike had to admit that he had lied to the American people, as well as to the Russians and the rest of the world. The spectacle of an American President behaving in such a bumbling way depressed most of his fellow citizens, but many of them were angry, too. Why hadn't their country been putting its scientific talent to better uses than developing this spy plane? How would Americans feel if Russia sent planes over the United States to photograph every airfield and military camp?

Still, nobody could stay angry at Ike as his final days in the White House approached. Some people even said that he probably could be elected again—if there weren't two compelling reasons against his running for a third term. After Franklin Roosevelt had shattered the tradition that limited any President to eight years in the White House, an amendment to the Constitution legally fixing the two-term limit had been adopted. Furthermore, Ike already was older than any other President, with health problems that could no longer be blinked away.

On October 14, 1960, he celebrated his seventieth birthday, and he looked his age even though his grin had not faded a bit. But by now, people of every political persuasion could salute him without any partisan feeling. For two other men were now engaged in a bitter contest to succeed him. Vice President Richard Nixon was running on the Republican ticket, opposing the Democratic Senator John F. Kennedy of Massachusetts.

As a convinced Republican, President Eisenhower naturally hoped Nixon would win—but Ike did not help him much. Because Nixon was insisting that he was better qualified than his opponent owing to his high-level experience in the government during his two terms as Vice President, a reporter at a press conference asked Eisenhower for an example of some important decision Nixon had helped to make.

Eisenhower thought a minute, then shrugged. "If you give me a week," he said, "I might think of one."

Yet during the final weeks of the campaign Ike went on a trip through several states, urging people to vote for Nixon. If only Ike had done more speaking, some people said, Nixon might have won the closest election in the nation's history—instead of losing by barely 100,000 votes.

When Kennedy won, Ike told friends he felt terribly disappointed. But soon the youngest man ever elected came calling on the oldest man ever to occupy the White House. Besides presenting photographers with a wonderful picture-taking opportunity, the visit gave Eisenhower a chance to console himself. The "young whippersnapper," as he privately described the forty-three-year-old Kennedy, seemed to him remarkably quick in grasping the scope of the problems he'd be confronting in just a few months.

Before leaving the White House for good, President Eisenhower offered the whole nation some thoughtful words of advice. Following an example set by George Washington, Eisenhower delivered a farewell address, in which he sounded an unexpected warning—voiced in spite of his own military background and his strong feelings in favor of spending billions for weapons. The country, he said, faced a new and dangerous problem.

During recent years, the United States had acquired "an immense military establishment" and "a large arms industry," he pointed out. "We recognize the imperative need for this development," he said. Then he went on:

> Yet we must not fail to comprehend its grave implications. . . . In the councils of government we must guard against the acquisition of unwarranted influence, whether sought or unsought, by the military-industrial complex. The potential for the disastrous rise of misplaced power exists and will persist. We must never let the weight of this combination endanger our liberties or democratic processes. We should take nothing for granted.

Satisfied, then, that he had shared his misgivings about the "military-industrial complex" with his fellow citizens, Dwight Eisenhower left Washington to relax on his farm in Pennsylvania.

14 BACK ON THE FARM

It turned out that Eisenhower had another nine years in which to reflect on his long life of public service. As he thought over his career, he came to feel that if history chose to remember him, it would be mainly for his role as Supreme Commander of the Allied forces in Europe during World War II.

And there was one accomplishment after he became President that he was proudest of. "The United States never lost a soldier or a foot of ground in my administration," he told an interviewer who sought him out at Gettysburg.

While he relaxed there, playing golf as often as his health permitted and enjoying the company of old friends, Ike's contributions also were being assessed by his fellow citizens. Most people predicted that three measures he had sponsored would be linked with his name in the future: the laws granting statehood to

Alaska and Hawaii, and the law establishing the interstate highway system.

But almost everybody seemed to agree with him that his war service would be his main claim to future fame. As the years passed, though, more and more people decided that he also deserved great credit for keeping the peace throughout his two terms in the White House.

He had refused time and again to be drawn into a shooting war, they said. Even when generals and admirals urged him to take steps that must lead to open conflict, he would not let them convince him. Only a man with his distinguished military career could have restrained the Pentagon's hotheads in the Cold War period when Eisenhower was President, according to this viewpoint.

Yet others did not agree. Dwight Eisenhower was wise to refuse to send American soldiers to help the French in Indochina in the 1950s, these people granted. He was wiser still, they said, to refuse to send atom bombs, despite the urging of many of his own aides. However, he had sent money to buy equipment for the French, who were fighting to keep Indochina as a colony. And when the French surrendered, he had sent millions more to "anti-Communists" in the three countries that had formerly comprised Indochina—Laos, Cambodia, and Vietnam.

Then, while Eisenhower was still in the White House,

The Eisenhowers at their Gettysburg farm.

several hundred "military advisors" had been sent to Vietnam. So it was Eisenhower who had taken the first step into the conflict in Southeast Asia, which was to have such a terrible impact as one President after another vastly increased the United States commitment in that far-off land.

The war in Vietnam was reaching its peak of fury when former President Eisenhower suffered a series of severe heart attacks in 1968. But from all over the country, thousands of cards and letters testified that Ike was still one of America's greatest heroes. People everywhere, regardless of their political feelings, poured forth a torrent of get-well wishes.

And, amazingly, he seemed to be recovering. Then another attack finally ended his life on March 28, 1969, six months short of his seventy-ninth birthday. After solemn ceremonies in Washington, attended by high officials from dozens of nations, a special train departed for Kansas, carrying the most famous citizen of the town of Abilene home to his final resting place.

SUGGESTED FOR FURTHER READING

The books listed here are suggested for young readers who may want to find out more about some of the leading figures and great events mentioned in DWIGHT EISENHOWER. It should be noted that this book is based mainly on Eisenhower's memoirs and other material from the Dwight D. Eisenhower Library in Abilene, Kansas. I would like to thank the staff there, particularly Acting Director Don W. Wilson, for their very kind help.

Bliven, Bruce. *From Casablanca to Berlin*. New York: Random House, 1965.

Faber, Doris. *Franklin Delano Roosevelt*. New York: Abelard-Schuman, 1975.

——. *Harry Truman*. New York: Abelard-Schuman, 1972.

Millis, Walter. *These Are the Generals*. New York: Knopf, 1943.

Mueller, Betty Jean. *The Dwight D. Eisenhower Library*. New York: Meredith, 1966.

Reeder, Red. *The Story of the Second World War*. New York: Hawthorn, 1970.

INDEX

ABOUT THE AUTHOR

Doris Faber was born in New York City and received her B.A. degree from New York University. She has worked as a free-lance writer and as a reporter for *The New York Times*. She is also the author of more than twenty biographies for young readers.

Mrs. Faber and her husband, Harold, a writer and editor, live in Ancram, New York. Since their children have grown up, they spend a good deal of their time (when they are not writing) restoring their splendid Victorian house and growing a vegetable garden.